Budding Poets

A Beginner's Guide to Verse and Rhyme

Written by Jessica Ashworth

Teaching & Learning Company

a Lorenz company

P.O. Box 802 Dayton, OH 45401-0802

www.LorenzEducationalPress.com

Table of Contents

TLC10605

How to Use This Book

Budding Poets is many things. It is a collection of original poetry for young students. It is a set of language arts activities for early writers. Most of all, it is a doorway to the discovery of the incredible power of words and language, and a key for children to unlock their amazing creative spirit.

Poetry can be a difficult subject for early learners. Its various forms, styles, and tools can be overwhelming to a young mind (or an older mind, for that matter). This is an important thing to remember as you present these units to your students. Equally important to consider, however, are the breathtaking powers and the adaptability of a developing mind. What better time to instill creative skills? And with what better subject to approach them? Despite its many aspects, at its heart, poetry is pure and free creation. When a child writes a line of poetry, he or she need not consider rules, formulas, or definitions. All they need do is express themselves. Once this concept is understood, specific forms and styles can be introduced, and a student can expand his or her knowledge and repertoire of poetry.

Budding Poets will help you with this in new and exciting ways. Each unit is based around a poetry skill or type, and features two levels of presentation and development – low and high. First, on low-level pages, a skill or type of poetry is introduced. Students are taken through a step-by-step process of creation and shown the results. Low-level activities approach the skill or poetry type from a simpler and creative angle, giving those new to the genre a chance to understand and build creative and poetic skills.

Next, high-level pages introduce and display to students some of the more advanced possibilities of poetry skills and types. High-level activities reinforce skills and offer a chance for students to begin shaping and writing their own poems. Each unit is concluded with a page of extension activities. These suggestions can extend the life and value of any unit through fun and challenging exercises, all focused on the continued discovery and development of creative and poetry skills.

The Poet's Toolbox introduces language arts concepts frequently used in poetry, such as different types of figurative language. *The Poet's Toolbox* will give students plenty of tools they can use to enhance their poems, but need not be presented before they start writing. Please note that some skills do not possess low and high presentations, though all feature low and high activities.

Poetry types are offered in alphabetical order. Low- and high-level presentations begin each unit, followed by low- and high-level activities. You might copy all low- or high-level pages and distribute them to students, or you might hand out an entire unit at once. You might also walk through presentations and activities as a class, on an overhead or interactive whiteboard. Extension activity pages are written to the teacher and should not be distributed to students.

It's important to note that this book has been written to students, even if it will be channeled through you, the teacher or parent. This means that any page, low or high, can begin or extend a study of poetry, whatever a student's age or experience.

No matter when or how you use *Budding Poets*, your students will discover the creative writer within themselves and begin expressing their personalities, emotions, and ideas through words and language. These are skills they will use and appreciate throughout their lives. It's never too early to teach that!

The Poet's Toolbox

Metaphor

ALLITERATION

Onomatopoeia

Personification

TLC10605

Alliteration
Low Level

Alliteration happens when two or more words in a row begin with the same letter or sound.

1. Let's create alliteration. First, think of any word. Write it down.

    brown

2. Now, all you have to do to make alliteration is to think of another word that begins with the same letter. Let's try writing a word that starts with the letter **B** and is something that is brown.

    brown **b**urger

3. There you have it: alliteration! You can add more words beginning with the same letter to make your alliteration more interesting or specific. Alliteration can be tricky when it comes to letters like X, Y, or Z, but dictionaries can help.

More Alliterations

chocolate **c**hips

french **f**ries

tan **t**oast

warm **w**ater

Alliteration
High Level

Alliteration is a poetry tool that uses repeated letters or sounds in words. The words are often in a row, but they don't need to be. Alliteration can give your poems personality and rhythm. While it's easiest to create alliterations using the same letters, you can also use similar sounds. Here are some examples: city and seat; food and phone; and quiet and couch.

Brenda **b**uttered **br**ead for **br**eakfast.

Carl's **c**ookie **c**ost a **c**ouple **q**uarters.

Harry **h**eld **h**is **h**ot **h**ot dog with one **h**and.

Sarah **s**lurped **c**ereal from her **s**poon.

Joe **d**rank **j**uice from a **j**ug.

TLC10605

Alliteration

Look at the items on each shelf. One doesn't belong! Say the name of each food out loud. Cross out the item that begins with a different letter or sound.

Alliteration

Look at the word magnets below. Use them to write three alliterative sentences on the blank lines provided. An example has been completed for you.

Example: Percy's playmate Peter plays piano.

1. _____

   _____

   _____

2. _____

   _____

   _____

3. _____

   _____

   _____

TLC10605

Extension Activities

1. Assign a different letter of the alphabet (or a sound) to each student. Have (or help) students cut out images and words from magazines that start with their assigned letter or sound. Use images and words to complete an alliterative alphabet poster to hang in the classroom. Younger students may need help with letters like Q, X, Y, and Z.

2. Write sets of alliterative words on index cards. Do this for at least three different letters or sounds. Shuffle the cards and have students organize them into alliterative categories.

3. Assign each student a letter of the alphabet. Have them write an alliterative sentence using that letter. Provide dictionaries or other reference materials for assistance. Students should read their completed sentences aloud.

4. Have students sit in a circle. Starting with the letter A, have students say aloud words that begin with that specific letter. Go around the circle until a student can't think of another word that begins with A. Then move to the letter B and continue through the alphabet.

5. Create several alliterative phrases. Write them on the board, leaving some words out. Go around the room and let students guess the missing words, one at a time.

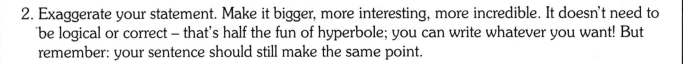

Hyperbole
Low/High Level

Hyperbole (hi-per-buh-lee) is making something seem bigger, faster, stronger, prettier, or better than it really is. You might not remember a simple line of poetry about a tall tree, but if that tree is taller than the world's highest mountain, you'll think about it later!

1. First, decide what you want to say.

   She talked fast.

Pretty boring, right? Let's see what we can do about that.

2. Exaggerate your statement. Make it bigger, more interesting, more incredible. It doesn't need to be logical or correct – that's half the fun of hyperbole; you can write whatever you want! But remember: your sentence should still make the same point.

   She talked a hundred miles an hour.

This sentence is much more interesting, but it still says that the woman talked quickly. By using hyperbole, we made the sentence more fun and memorable. Making simple statements better is very important in poetry.

More Hyperbole

This room is a mess.
Hyperbole: This room looks like a tornado hit it.

You're too loud!
Hyperbole: You're going to wake the dead!

He is big.
Hyperbole: He is bigger than an ox.

I am tired.
Hyperbole: I could sleep for a year.

TLC10605

Hyperbole

Write the letter for the correct statement next to each hyperbole.

Hyperboles

_____ This desk belonged to a cave man.

_____ Her eyes are the size of the moon.

_____ His brain is so big he can't wear a hat.

_____ I've gone a million miles in these shoes.

_____ That dog can outrun a plane!

Statements

A. He is smart.

B. The dog is fast!

C. She has big eyes.

D. This desk is old.

E. These shoes are worn out.

Hyperbole

Choose two words from the bank below to complete each hyperbole.

high	eyes
coconuts	snowman
cold	mirror
sun	stare
hungry	looking
mouth	kitchen

I was so _____ I ate the _____ .

I was so _____ I felt like a _____ .

I can break a _____ just by _____ at it.

If you _____ too long, your _____ will fall out.

The kite is so _____ it's made friends with the _____ .

You could fit at least five _____ in your _____ .

TLC10605

Extension Activities

1. Hand out several sentences to students and allow them to craft their own hyperboles for each.

2. Break students into small groups. Instruct each group to brainstorm hyperboles about each member's physical features or characteristics. For example: *Jon has flaming red hair.*

3. Read students a passage that includes several hyperboles. Ask students to count the number of hyperboles they hear and then discuss them.

4. Reinforce the concept of exaggeration by telling a tall tale as a class. Have students sit in a circle. Begin telling a story full of exaggerated characters, settings, and plot developments. After a couple minutes, pass the story to the student on your right. Ask students to continue the story using as much exaggeration as possible. Students can talk for as little or as long as they want.

5. Read sentences to your students. Have students decide whether each is a hyperbole or not. For sentences that are not hyperboles, have students brainstorm ways to hyperbolize them.

Metaphor
Low/High Level

A metaphor is a comparison of two different things that are alike in some way. These two things might not seem similar at first; a metaphor can connect them in new and creative ways. Don't confuse metaphors with similes (see page xx). You can be sure it's a metaphor if the comparison doesn't use the words *like* or *as*.

1. To create a metaphor, you must start with an idea. What are you trying to express? A good place to start is by describing a person.

    Joe is grumpy in the morning.

Now let's use metaphor to better describe Joe.

2. Think of a different way of expressing your idea. Relate it to something else. When Joe gets up in the morning, he frowns and grumbles a lot. He doesn't like to talk or be bothered, and he yells if he's disturbed. Hey, that gives me an idea!

    Joe is a bear in the morning.

By comparing Joe's grumpiness to a shaggy, roaring bear, we've created a metaphor. This would work much better in a poem.

More Metaphors

Grandma is a good person.
Metaphor: Grandma has a heart of gold.

Sarah is very happy.
Metaphor: Sarah is glowing.

The home team is winning.
Metaphor: The home team is on fire.

This store is confusing.
Metaphor: This store is a maze.

14

Metaphor

Circle the metaphors in the sentence pairs below.

The moon lights the sky.   The moon is a flashlight.

I am a turtle.   I am a slow walker.

My brother is hairy.   My brother is an animal.

Your hands are rough.   Your hands are sandpaper.

Sandy is a lobster.   Sandy has sunburn.

This room is an oven.   This room is warm.

Metaphor

Based on each pair of words, write a metaphor on the line provided. Add necessary words so the metaphor makes sense.

bunny, ball

_____

purse, rocks

_____

sand, sugar

_____

Fill in the blanks to complete the metaphor. Use the hints if needed.

The _____ was a bird in the sky.
(Filled with air; A string for a tail)

The _____ was a painting for the garden.
(Grows from a seed; Smells nice)

The _____ was a blanket for the ground.
(Comes in the winter; White and cold)

TLC10605

Extension Activities

1. Make each Monday Metaphor Monday. Explain that students should think of traits that describe each of them. Then each student should decide on a metaphor reflecting that trait. *For example: You might be a magician for one Monday, because you know all the tricks to getting an A. One student might be a cheetah, because she is the fastest on her community soccer team.*

2. Share a poem on the board. Have students either count the number of metaphors in the poem or write the metaphors on a piece of paper.

3. Write nonsensical metaphors on the board. *Example: That cat looks like a train whistle.* Have students volunteer to circle the incorrect information in the metaphor. As a class, correct the metaphor so it makes a sensible comparison.

4. Read metaphors and similes aloud to your students. Have students take turns deciding whether the sentence is a metaphor or simile (see page 18). If it is a metaphor, how can they change it to a simile (or vice versa)?

5. Divide your class into small groups. Hand each group an envelope filled with various pictures. Each envelope should have the same pictures. In an allotted amount of time groups should use the pictures to write as many metaphors as possible. Have each group share their metaphors with the class.

Simile
Low/High Level

A simile (sim-ill-ee) is a comparison of two different things that are alike in some way. These two things might not seem similar at first; a simile can connect them in new and creative ways. Similes are much like metaphors, but similes use the words *like* or *as*. This special poetry tool can be used to create a picture with words.

1. Start by deciding what idea you want to express.

   This cookie does not taste good.

2. That describes the taste of the cookie, but it doesn't do it strongly enough! Let's create a simile to really stress how bad the cookie tasted. Think of another thing that we can compare the cookie to, something that will express its bad taste. Remember: you must use *like* or *as*.

   This cookie tastes **like** dirt!

That's better. This simile would work well in a poem because it expresses an idea that a reader would remember.

More Similes

This floor is slippery.
Simile: This floor is as slick as ice.

John's face is red.
Simile: John's face looks like a cherry.

Grandpa has dark eyes.
Simile: Grandpa's eyes are as dark as night.

The thorns are sharp.
Simile: The thorns are like knives.

18

Simile

Decide whether each sentence is a simile or not a simile. Write a letter S if the sentence is a simile. Write a letter N if it is not.

_____ The leaves are all over the ground.   _____ That bell is ringing.

_____ The leaves are falling like rain.   _____ Deer move like race cars.

_____ That bell is as loud as thunder.   _____ Deer run fast.

Simile

Unscramble each of the similes. Rewrite them on the lines below. Then write what each simile means.

is as big The sky ocean. as an

Simile: _____

Meaning: _____

move like Ballerinas the floor. across feathers

Simile: _____

Meaning: _____

sharp as Careful, the pencil is a tack.

Simile: _____

Meaning: _____

whistles like Your teapot train. a

Simile: _____

Meaning: _____

as Her Rudolph's. nose was red as

Simile: _____

Meaning: _____

like a dog He bites his chewing nails a bone.

Simile: _____

Meaning: _____

TLC10605

Extension Activities

1. Set up a Hangman game on your board. Give hints to your class through the use of similes. *For example: I am as cold as ice and white as a cloud (snow).* Let students guess letters until you complete the game.

2. Have each student write a noun on the board. Either as a class or individually, pair nouns to make silly or sensible similes.

3. Each student should pick an unfamiliar noun from the dictionary and write its definition on a piece of paper. With definitions in hand, take a short walk outside or around school. Ask each student to find something that compares with his or her noun, whether in color, shape, texture, weight, or any other similarity they discover. Students should write a simile comparing the two words upon returning to class.

4. Explain the concept of clichés to your students. Then provide a list of common ones. Encourage students to think creatively and rewrite some of the words to each simile, thus creating original comparisons.

5. Have pairs of students sift through old magazines searching for two images that compare in someway. Ask students to cut out images and write a simile illustrating the connection. Students may draw the images instead.

Onomatopoeia
Low/High Level

Onomatopoeia (on-oh-mot-uh-pee-uh) is a very big word. Its definition is much simpler. Onomatopoeia is using words to represent sounds. We're not talking about adjectives (loud, annoying, strange). When you use onomatopoeia, you actually give a sound its own word. For example:

Water *drips*.

If you've ever heard a leaking sink, you know that the sound of a drop of water really sounds like the word *drip*. Here's another example.

Balloons *pop*.

Get the idea? Onomatopoeia is a great poet tool because it shows a reader exactly what something sounds like. Instead of a loud noise, a poet might describe a *bang*, a *screech*, or a *wham*. This makes a poem more descriptive. The best thing about onomatopoeia is that it doesn't even have to be a real word. If you think something sounds like *ploom*, go ahead and write it!

More Onomatopoeia

Cars *rattle*.

Boots *stomp*.

Alarms *beep*.

Water *drips*.

Horns *honk*.

Balloons *pop*.

The bug *buzzes* in my ear.

Birds are *chirping* a pretty song.

The frog's *ribbit* is getting louder.

Watch out for *hissing* snakes.

The alligator *chomps* his jaws.

Dogs *howl* at the storm.

TLC10605

Onomatopoeia

Pair each sound with an animal that might make it.

Baa

Cluck

Meow

Oink

Roar

Woof

Onomatopoeia

The cars are *mooing* and the cows are *vrooming*! Cross out the incorrect sound words in each sentence. Write the correct word from the bank below on the line provided. There are some words in the bank that will not be used.

Pigs roar when they're happy.

_____

Someone's beeping on the door.

_____

Ow! I just hummed my head.

_____

The hen's gurgling kept me awake.

_____

Shh! Listen to the zap of the clock.

_____

Can you hear the rumble of the bacon frying?

_____

I hear the kitten's snort. She must be pleased!

_____

sizzle
meow
drip
baa
knocking
purr
swooshing
oink
whacked
tick-tock
clucking
poof
thud

TLC10605

Extension Activities

1. Pair up students for "I Say-You Say." One student says an animal noise, and the other student names the animal. For example: I say baa, you say (sheep); I say neigh, you say (horse).

2. Twist poster paper into the shape of a megaphone. Have students take turns making sounds with the megaphone. Whoever correctly names the source of the sound must use the sound in a sentence. Then that student takes his or her turn with the megaphone.

3. Have students craft a sound poem with an abcb rhyme pattern. Assign common sounds such as rain, thunder, applause, and laughter, as subjects.

4. Cut out animal or object images. Ask students to brainstorm all of the nouns the image could be. Then have students use onomatopoeia in a sentence.

5. Write a comic book story together. Explain the use of action sound words such as *boom, zap, bang,* and *buzz* in comics. Ask students to say aloud a sentence using this form of onomatopoeia. Write each sentence on the board. Then read your story aloud once the board is covered.

Personification
Low/High Level

Personification makes objects, things, or animals seem like humans.

1. First, describe something in a normal way.

   This rug is old.

   This tells us that the rug has been around for a while, but it doesn't really paint a picture.

2. Next, rewrite your description using a human characteristic. You should still express the same idea.

   This rug is exhausted.

That's more like it! You can picture an exhausted person. He or she might be bent over, breathing hard, looking pale and miserable. You might even know what it feels like to be exhausted. This gives us a much better description of just how old and beat-up the rug is.

More Personification

The vacuum does not work.
Personification: The vacuum is lazy.

My couch is big and comfortable.
Personification: My couch will swallow you!

The door makes a lot of noise.
Personification: The door has a lot to say.

The drain is making noise.
Personification: The drain has the hiccups.

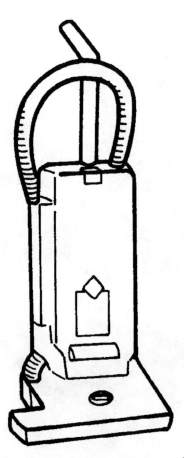

TLC10605

Personification

Draw a line from each sentence on the left to a sentence on the right that expresses the same idea. Draw a picture of one of the personifications in the box below.

My head is angry.	Hurricanes make the news.
The piano shouted for attention.	I have a headache.
Her phone begged to be answered.	Your plants need water.
Hurricanes are TV stars.	Her phone rang again and again.
Your plants are thirsty.	The piano was loud.

Personification

Use personification to complete the sentences. The first one has been completed for you.

My chapped lips are __shouting__ for help.

The stars were _____ of the fireworks.

How _____ the unread books must be.

A new lamp _____ lit the room.

The hot kernels _____ inside the bag.

The cat leapt onto the fence like a(n) _____ .

That tree branch looks like _____ .

_____ like a _____ , the airplane took to the sky.

The storm _____ as if it were a _____ .

The waterfall _____ over the cliff. It reminded me of a(n) _____ .

          TLC10605

Extension Activities

1. Show your students a picture of an object, animal, or thing. Then read them a human characteristic. Ask students to compose a sentence including the picture and human characteristic.

2. Assign each student a letter of the alphabet. Have students compose a sentence using personification and an illustration of the sentence. *For example: The ants compete to carry the heaviest load.* Help the students with X and Z, or leave those letters out.

3. Personify the classroom. Construct a list on the board of all the objects in the classroom. On a piece of paper, have each student personify at least two objects.

4. Gather odd objects in a box. Have each student grab an object from the box and personify it in three ways. Each student should share one personification with the class.

5. Devise a classroom scavenger hunt for your students. Divide students into groups and have them find the objects based on personification hints. *For example: I growl every time I chew your pencil to a point. Turn my handle too fast, and I might bite off the top!*

Types of Poetry

Lune

DIAMANTE

LYRICS

Occasional Poetry

Concrete Poetry

Tongue Twister

 Acrostic

 Couplets

Acrostic Poetry
Low Level

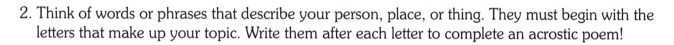

An acrostic poem describes a person, a place, or a thing. It uses words that begin with the letters of the word being described.

1. Think of a person, place, or thing about which to write. Write that word from top to bottom.

   B
   E
   A
   R

2. Think of words or phrases that describe your person, place, or thing. They must begin with the letters that make up your topic. Write them after each letter to complete an acrostic poem!

   Big paws
   Ears are small
   Always hungry
   Ready to sleep

More Acrostic Poems

Flames
In the air
Rising smoke
Everywhere

To sleep inside
Everyone is warm
No beds
Thick blankets

Acrostic Poetry
High Level

An acrostic poem describes a subject of your choice. Each line of the poem is about your subject. These lines begin with words that begin with the letters of your subject.

Can we tell ghost stories
And roast marshmallows?
Maybe some black bears will
Pass our tent tonight.
Is there a creek or pond
Nice enough to swim across?
Grab your suits and jump in!

TLC10605

Acrostic Poetry

Fill in each blank line with the word from the bank that correctly completes the acrostic poem.

B _____ my teeth.

L _____ are out.

A _____ ready for sleep.

N _____ to worry about.

K _____ tucked in tight.

E _____ to sleep.

T _____ Teddy good night.

keep
almost
nothing
lights
brushed
tell
excited

Acrostic Poetry

Look at the words below. For each letter, write a person, place, or thing that the acrostic's subject describes. Then draw a picture for one of your completed poems in the box below.

F _____

A _____

S _____

T _____

S _____

H _____

I _____

N _____

Y _____

Extension Activities

1. Have students write acrostics based on their friends' names.

2. Pick a classroom item, like chalk, and write an acrostic for it.

3. Write the following words on the board: CLASSROOM, LIBRARY, and RECESS. Write an acrostic for each, either together as a class or individually.

4. Show your class a picture of a famous landmark, like the Statue of Liberty or Mount Rushmore. Write an acrostic poem using the landmark's name. You can do this as a class, or assign it to students individually or in small groups.

5. Take your class for a walk. Ask students to write down five things they see during the walk. When you get back to the classroom, instruct students to write an acrostic for at least one of the things they listed.

Alphabet Poetry
Low Level

Alphabet poetry can be about anything. But it's a good idea to choose a topic that you can write lots of words about. Why? Because in order to write an alphabet poem, you need to write a word that begins with *every* letter of the alphabet!

1. Choose a topic that you want to write about. Try to pick something common or that you know a lot about. Let's write about a:

   Junk Drawer

2. Starting with the letter *A* and continuing all the way to *Z*, write words about your topic. When you have 26 words, your alphabet poem will be finished! Since we're writing about the junk drawer, let's write some things that are found in it.

   Acorn, **B**ead, **C**andy…

   Separate each word with a comma (,). Your alphabet poem can have as many lines as you like.

3. Don't worry if you have trouble thinking of words that begin with tricky letters like **X**, **Y**, or **Z**. Try looking for words in a dictionary, or ask an adult to give you some ideas.

Junk Drawer

Acorn, **B**ead, **C**andy, **D**ust
Eraser, **F**eathers, **G**lue,
Hair, **I**nk, **J**acks, **K**ite,
Lists, **M**ints, **N**otes, **O**dor,
Pictures, **Q**uarters, **R**ings,
Stamp, **T**in, **U**mbrella,
Vest, **W**atch, **X**-ray,
Yarn, **Z**ippers

TLC10605

Alphabet Poetry

High Level

Alphabet poems are made up of words that describe your chosen topic. You must have one word for every letter of the alphabet, arranged in order. If you have trouble with letters like X, Y, and Z, try using creative tricks like the poem below. Don't forget: a poet can write whatever he or she wants!

Sick Day

Achoo!, bellyache,
cough, doctor, earache,
fever, groggy,
headache,
icepack, juice, kisses, love,
movie, nap, oatmeal,
pillows, quilt,
restless, sneezing, tears,
upset,
vitamins, water,
eXhausted, yawn,
Zzzzz

Alphabet Poetry

Cut out the words below. Paste them in alphabetical order to make an alphabet poem.

The Zoo

Yak	Birds	Quiet
Elephant	Vicious	Otter
Wolf	Seals	Tigers
Insect	eXciting	Ugly
Rabbit	Ants	Panda
Ducks	Monkey	Lion
Jaguar	Cheetahs	Zebra
Noisy	Hippo	Kangaroo
Giraffe	Flamingo	

TLC10605

Alphabet Poetry

Fill in the blanks below with words that fit the alphabet poem's title. Some have been provided for you. Use a dictionary or other reference material if you need help. Remember, alphabet poems have a word for every letter of the alphabet, arranged in order.

The Mall

Advertisements, _____, _____,

_____, _____,

Food, _____, _____,

_____, _____,

Kites, _____, _____,

_____, _____,

Posters, _____, _____,

_____, _____,

Undershirts, _____, _____,

_____, _____,

_____

Extension Activities

1. Go around the room and have each student say their first name aloud. Write each name on the board. As you go, let students tell you where the names should appear to keep the list in alphabetical order. Have students call out names for any letters that aren't used. For older students, try letting each person write his or her name on the board in the correct alphabetical position. You might also have students organize both first and last names.

2. Have students write a backwards alphabet poem beginning with the letter Z. Let them choose their own topics.

3. Let students go on an alphabet scavenger hunt. Starting with A, they should find an item in the classroom that begins with each letter of the alphabet. Have them record their objects on a sheet of paper. Make sure you bring in a few objects for difficult letters, like X and Z.

4. Bring some music to class and play it for students. Let students call out topics that the music makes them think about. Choose a topic as a class and write an alphabet poem together.

5. Make an alphabet poem collage as a class or individually. Students should look through magazines and newspapers for pictures and/or words of items or people that begin with each letter of the alphabet. Hang the finished collages around the classroom.

TLC10605

Catalog Poetry
Low Level

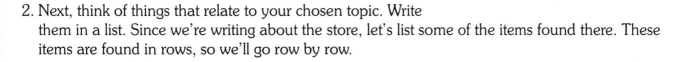

A catalog is a list of items that fit in a group. A catalog poem is made up of lines about the same topic.

1. First, decide what you want to catalog. It should be something from which you can make a list. It could be anything: a person, a place, or an adventure. This will be the focus of your catalog poem. Let's write about an adventure:

    a trip to the store

2. Next, think of things that relate to your chosen topic. Write them in a list. Since we're writing about the store, let's list some of the items found there. These items are found in rows, so we'll go row by row.

    This row has cheese and milk.
    This row has ketchup and mustard.
    This row has bread and chips.

3. Keep writing things about your topic. Your list can be as long or short as you like. Now you have a catalog! Organize your catalog into lines. You can add lines before and after your catalog to make your poem more interesting or clear.

A Trip to the Store

There are eight rows at the grocery store.
This row has cheese and milk.
This row has ketchup and mustard.
This row has bread and chips.
This row has cereal and cookies.
This row has noodles and crackers.
This row has potatoes and tomatoes.
This row has bananas and apples.
This row…this row has candy bars and gum!
Please, may I have one?

Catalog Poetry
High Level

Catalog poems are lists about a specific topic. They can be so much more than simple lists, however. By listing a complete set of events, for example, you can tell a story or describe an event. You can also add specific details to your listed items to paint a vivid picture for your readers. Try to *show* your topic through descriptive language.

At the Races

The stands are full of people.
The people are cheering for the drivers.
The drivers are sitting in their cars.
The cars are going around in circles.
The circle track is covered in dirt.
The dirt is flying into my eyes.
My eyes follow the lead car.
The leading car wins the race.
The race ends with the checkered flag.

Once a Year

I eat warm pancakes for breakfast.
I watch silly animal cartoons.
I splash blue pool water on my sister.
I swim in circles until I'm tired.
I wear my new striped shirt.
I listen to my family sing loudly.
I blow out hot candles and wish for a puppy.
I rip the paper and ribbon of each present.
I say thank you, thank you, and thank you.
I choose the biggest piece of vanilla cake.
I fall asleep and dream of next year's birthday.

TLC10605

Catalog Poetry

Draw a line from each catalog poem to its correct title.

Wake up early
Pack my backpack
Sit at my desk

Saturdays

My Dog

Are funny
Are smart
Are helpful

My Friends

Is friendly
Is soft
Is fast

Mondays

Watch cartoons
Eat pancakes
Play games

Catalog Poetry

Decide in which catalog poem each sentence below belongs. Rewrite the sentences under the proper titles in correct order.

Now lift yourself on top of the branch.
Hold the stone like a Frisbee.
Find a place for your toe.
Squat down close to the shore.
Rest before climbing higher!
Start with a flat and smooth stone.
Aim just above the water and throw!
Start by grabbing the lowest branch by both hands.

How to Climb a Tree

_____.

_____.

_____.

_____.

How to Skip a Rock

_____.

_____.

_____.

_____.

TLC10605

Extension Activities

1. Have students write an "Around the Classroom" or an "In My Desk" catalog and then revise it to create a catalog poem.

2. Brainstorm how-to topics on the board, such as "How to Clean My Room" or "How to Build a Fort." Have students write a how-to catalog poem for each topic.

3. Show students the cover of an unfamiliar book. Ask them to write a catalog poem based on what they imagine the book would be about.

4. Supply each student with a magazine. Allow students time to look through the pages. Instruct them to write a title for a catalog poem based on the magazine. Then ask students to cut out images and words based on their title. Collage the clippings to complete the catalog poem.

5. Let students take turns standing in front of the class and announcing a catalog poem title and two additional lines. *For example: I'm going to an amusement park. I'm bringing sunscreen. I'm wearing tennis shoes.* What else would we take to an amusement park? Have the seated students volunteer their answers.

Clerihew
Low Level

A clerihew is a poem about a person. It has four lines that tell about the person. The first and second lines rhyme with one another. The third and fourth lines rhyme, too, but not with the first two lines. This is called an *aabb rhyme scheme.*

1. First, write down a name. It can be real or made up. Finding rhyme words for names can be tricky, so you can use a first or last name.

    Joey Glow

2. Write a line about the person whose name you chose. You might describe how he or she looks, or you can write about what the person acts like. The last word in this line must rhyme with your chosen name. This creates your *aa rhyme.*

Joey Glow	(a)
Had skin white as snow.	(a)

3. Write two more lines about your chosen person. They must rhyme with one another. This creates your *bb rhyme.* Remember that you're trying to tell readers about your person. When you have four lines, your clerihew is finished!

Joey Glow	(a)
Had skin white as snow.	(a)
He looked like glue,	(b)
But his eyes were blue.	(b)

More Clerihews

Holly Bird	(a)
Didn't know a word.	(a)
She could chirp and fly,	(b)
But never said hi.	(b)

Chris Crunch	(a)	Betty Boat	(a)
Ate rocks for lunch.	(a)	Was able to float.	(a)
His teeth were so strong	(b)	She lived on the sea,	(b)
He munched all day long.	(b)	Where she could float free.	(b)

TLC10605

Clerihew

High Level

Clerihews are four-line poems about a person written in an *aabb rhyme scheme*. They begin with a name on the first line. The remaining three lines describe that person. Clerihews are often strange or funny poems about made-up people. Try to write lines that provide a snapshot of your person.

Jasper Monroe   (a)
Looked much like a toe.   (a)
He did not care   (b)
When people stopped to stare.   (b)

Sheila No Frown   (a)
Stayed dressed as a clown.   (a)
She raced from party to party   (b)
So she would never be tardy.   (b)

Gary Grump
Hit his knee with a *thump*.
He screamed out in pain
Now he walks with a cane.

Dolly Blue Eyes
Told lots of lies.
Said she went to the moon
On a big silver spoon.

Clerihew

Fill in the blanks with words from the bank to complete the clerihews.

Benny Ball

Was round and _____

He rolled away

When it was time to _____

Sarah Smell

Sang like a _____

She had roses to eat

So her breath would be _____

| small |
| thin |
| sweet |
| bell |
| jar |
| white |
| pop |
| play |

Barry Big Grin

Was tall and _____

His eyes were bright

And his teeth were _____

Susan Gold Star

Lived in a _____

She shot to the top

But the lid wouldn't _____

Clerihew

Unscramble the clerihews and rewrite them in correct order on the lines provided.

She tried to shout,

Rita Ray

Had nothing to say.

But nothing came out

For his beautiful tune

That made others swoon

Was known around town

Birdy Brown

Jonny Stop Staring

His *eyes* were blurry and red,

Had a habit of glaring.

As he never put them to bed

Willy Watch Out

He uncovered crimes and lies

While in perfect disguise

Was a private scout.

_____

_____

_____

_____

_____

_____

_____

_____

_____

_____

_____

_____

_____

_____

_____

_____

Extension Activities

1. Have students write clerihews using their names.

2. Ask students to create new names for themselves and to assign their new selves a super power. Once each has decided a name and a power, write a clerihew to share with the class. Start an ABC wall with student's clerihews. Include pictures from magazines, or have students draw pictures of characters.

3. Divide the class into groups of four students. Seat groups in circles around the classroom. Each group should pick one of its members to go first. He or she should start by saying his or her name aloud. The next student in the circle should supply a line about that person that rhymes with the first student's name. The third student should add a line about the first, and the fourth should rhyme his or her final line with the third. In this way, groups will create organic clerihews. Groups should compose a clerihew for each member.

4. Provide students with pictures of people, famous or unknown. Have students choose a person to write a clerihew about.

5. Have students create a Clerihew Kit. Provide each student with eight index cards and an empty bag. Instruct them to write the following (one to each card): two names, two nouns or verbs that rhyme with the names, and two additional pairs of rhyming nouns or verbs. Have students place all cards into their bags. Place all of the bags on a table. One at a time, students should choose a bag (making sure it isn't their own). Have each student use the word cards in his or her Clerihew Kit to write two clerihews.

TLC10605

Concrete Poetry

Low Level

Concrete poetry is poetry you can actually *see*! That's because the poem takes the shape of what it's about. The poem's subject is described in a way that looks like the idea being described. Let's take a look.

1. First, decide what you want to write about. It's easier to start with a simple or common subject. For example, let's write a concrete poem about a book bag.

2. Since the special thing about concrete poetry is the way the poem looks, let's draw a picture of the book bag next.

3. Now that we have a picture of our subject, we can focus on the poetry. We want to describe the book bag, so let's write some lines about it.

   My book bag is blue with yellow dots.
   Inside are my pencils, erasers, and folders.

4. Once you've created your poem's lines, you must write them in or on your subject's picture. There isn't a right or wrong place for your lines, so be as creative as you can! After you've finished writing your lines, step back and have a look at your concrete poem.

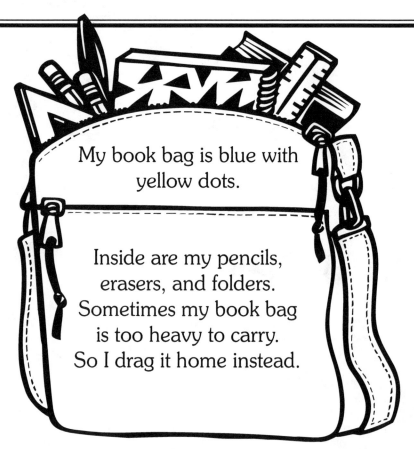

My book bag is blue with yellow dots.

Inside are my pencils, erasers, and folders. Sometimes my book bag is too heavy to carry. So I drag it home instead.

Concrete Poetry
High Level

Concrete poetry takes the shape of what it's about. The poem's subject is described in a way that looks like the idea being described. Perhaps a poem about a wheel will be written in a circle, or a poem about a home will be written inside a drawing of the house. The important idea is to symbolize the poem's topic in both words and pictures.

Is my lunch box packed? peanut butter crackers is my favorite. inside. note is and juice, or sandwich turkey and cheese and milk. A Look! A What's inside? I hope I have cookies

Concrete Poetry

Draw a line from each set of lines to the concrete poetry picture in which they could be written.

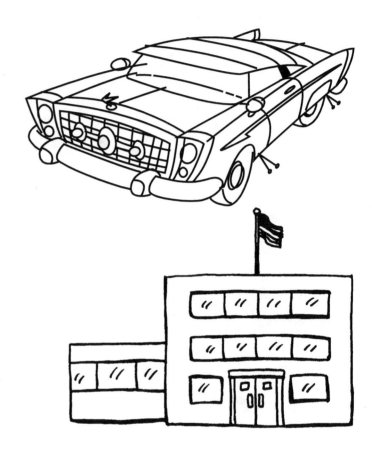

Bouncing up and down,
On a wooden **court**.
An **orange ball** takes flight
And swishes through a **hoop**.

My **engine** roars.
My **tires** spin.
I **toot** my horn
As my **driver** gets in.

When the **bell** rings,
Boys and **girls** jump up.
They leave the **desks** behind,
Forgetting **tests** and **books**.

Concrete Poetry

Fill in the concrete poetry templates below. You can write full sentences or descriptive words.

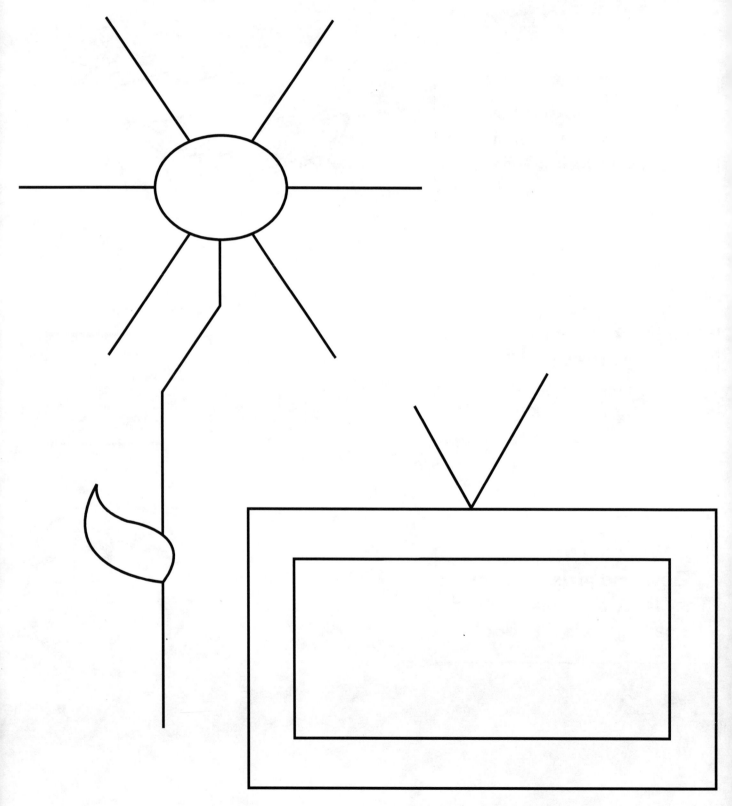

Extension Activities

1. Place a concrete poem template on display. Let students call out words or phrases and build a poem to fit the template.

2. Let students choose objects from around the classroom to write concrete poems about.

3. Have students trace their hands on a piece of construction paper. Have them write concrete poems about themselves or how they use their hands at school and at home.

4. Bring several coloring books to class. Let students pick their favorite pictures and trace them on a piece of paper. Then have students write poems inside or on the traced lines of the picture.

5. Divide the class into groups. Hand out sets of index cards with lists of related words on them. For example, hand out a list of things that could be found in a refrigerator. Let students devise a shape and arrange the words in a concrete poem.

Couplets
Low Level

A couplet is made up of two lines that rhyme. Writing couplets is a great way to practice poetry!

1. What do you want to write about? Your couplet can be about anything – a person, an object, or even an idea. How about the sun?

2. Once you've decided on a topic, write your first line of poetry about that topic. Remember that you will have to rhyme with your last word. Don't pick anything too difficult!

   Summer sun

3. Finish your couplet by writing a second line about your topic that rhymes with the first.

   Summer sun
   Time for fun

4. Once you have the hang of writing couplets, you can try writing an entire poem of couplets. All you have to do is write several couplets about the same topic.

Seasons

Summer sun,
Time for fun.

The leaves are brown
When they fall down.

Winter brings snow,
Nothing can grow.

The colors come out
When spring is about.

The clouds are big and white
The sun is out of sight.

As snow covers the ground,
It falls without a sound.

Watch the moving trees,
Here comes a cold breeze.

The sun is melting the ice,
And again it will be nice.

56

Couplets
High Level

Couplets are pairs of rhyming lines. Sometimes, a couplet expresses a complete thought by itself.

> The wind is moving fast and the trees are bending.
> Everyone run inside, for the storm isn't ending.

Several couplets can also be used to form a longer poem. Notice how each couplet adds to the greater subject or theme of the poem.

From Dark to Light

The wind is moving fast and the trees are bending.
Everyone run inside, for the storm isn't ending.

After the rain, as the sun begins to show,
Look to the sky, and you might see a rainbow.

The sun is setting and it will soon be night.
After many dark hours, it will again be light.

The birds are chirping, so it must be morning.
They wake me each day with a quiet warning.

Couplets

Draw a line from each word to a picture that rhymes with it. The first one has been completed for you.

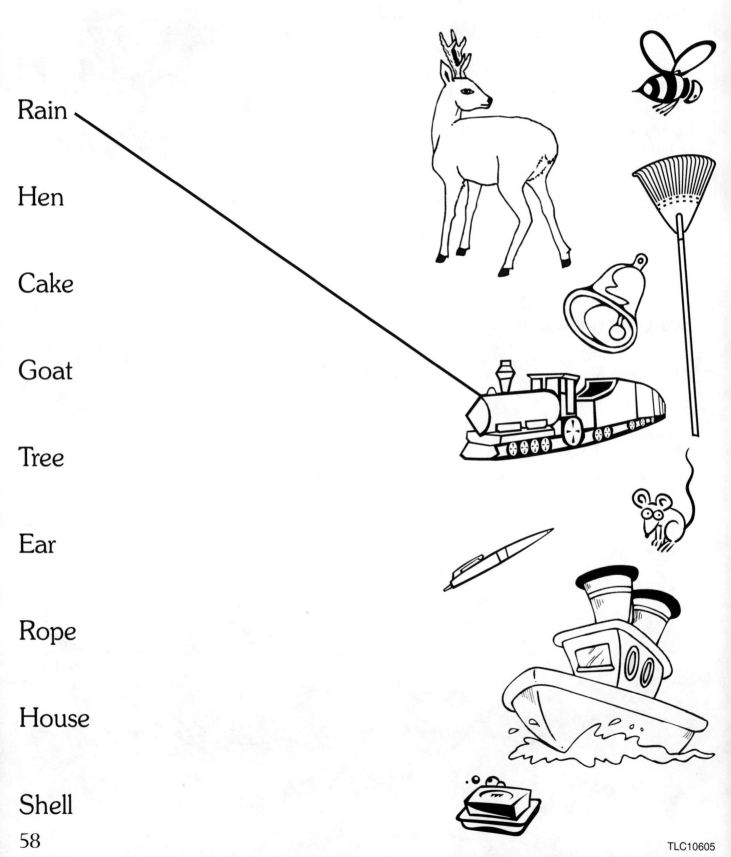

Rain

Hen

Cake

Goat

Tree

Ear

Rope

House

Shell

Name _____   Date _____

Couplets

Fill in the blanks to complete the couplets.

The ball is flying through the _____,

As the fans in the stands stop to _____.

The goalie stands in front of the _____.

It's starting to rain, so the ball will be _____.

The runner ran fast around the _____.

He's in the front, but he started in the _____.

The tennis player hits the ball with a mighty _____.

If he wins this match, they'll crown him _____.

The hockey puck slips and slides on the _____.

The home team scored once, can they do it _____?

Extension Activities

1. Discuss the concept of cause and effect with students. Write several causes on the board. For each cause, have students write a rhyming effect. For example: Cause - *If Susan gives the table a hard shake*; Effect - *the priceless vase might fall off and break.*

2. Break students into pairs. Have one student begin by saying a sentence. The second student should respond with a sentence that forms a couplet. Students can reverse roles and continue. Have each pair decide on a favorite couplet to share with the class.

3. Play *I Spy Couplets* with your class. Start by giving students two clues in the form of a couplet. For example: *I spy something we use to write. It is soft and white. (Chalk)* The student that first answers correctly should supply the next couplet clue.

4. Have each student open a dictionary to a random page. Instruct each to choose a word from the page and write a couplet using that word. Have each student write his or her couplet on the board to share the new words with the other students.

5. Choose a word unfamiliar to your students. Write it on the board. Have students take turns writing rhyming words on the board. As a class compose a series of couplets using the rhyming words.

60

Diamante

Low Level

A diamante (dee-uh-mon-tay) is a poem in the shape of a diamond. It has this shape because each line has a specific number of words. Diamantes are always about nouns. They are written in a pattern.

1. Before you pick a noun for your diamante, you should know the pattern:

        noun
        2 adjectives about noun
        3 –ing verbs about noun
        4 words about noun
        3 –ing verbs about noun
        2 adjectives about noun
        noun

2. Now, pick a noun about which to write. This word will be the first and last lines of your poem. Everything between will be about that word, so make sure to pick something about which you can write a lot. For example, you might write about a family member.

    Grandma

3. Next, fill in the lines of your poem **according to the pattern**. Remember that you're describing the noun you chose with every adjective and verb. Try to write the most important things about that person, place, or thing.

Grandma

Grandma
Kind, wise
Loving, teaching, protecting
Proud of her family
Cooking, sewing, tidying
Graceful, just
Grandma

Diamante
High Level

Diamantes are poems written in specific patterns. When they're completed, they resemble diamonds in their shape. Diamantes are always about nouns. Some (see page 31) describe a single noun. Others, like the one below, describe two opposite nouns. These diamantes have a specific pattern, too:

noun (1)
2 adjectives about noun (1)
3 –ing verbs about noun (1)
2 adjectives about noun(1) – two adjectives about noun (2)
3 –ing verbs about noun (2)
2 adjectives about noun (2)
noun (2) – the opposite of noun (1)

This kind of diamante shows the differences between two nouns. By focusing on specific words about the nouns, diamantes express a lot in little space.

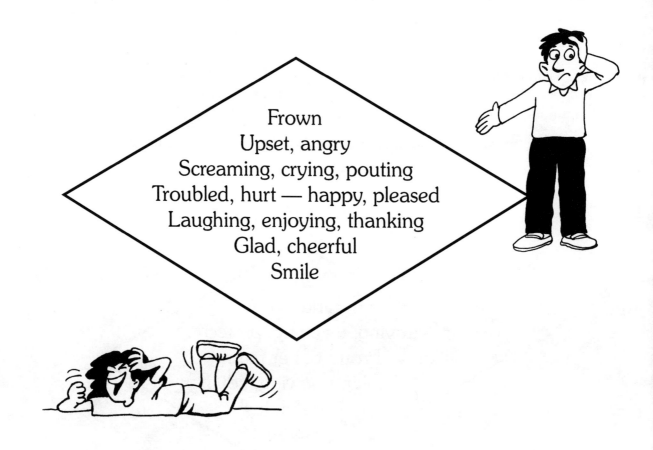

Frown
Upset, angry
Screaming, crying, pouting
Troubled, hurt — happy, pleased
Laughing, enjoying, thanking
Glad, cheerful
Smile

Diamante

Cut out the lines below. Arrange them in correct order to form a diamante. Rewrite the diamante on another piece of paper. Decorate the poem with pictures.

Reading, talking, thinking

Tired, excited

Young, curious

Student

Pupil

Doing what is best

Playing, writing, asking

Diamante

Complete the diamante chart below based on a subject of your choice. Once you've completed the chart, write and decorate your diamante on a piece of construction paper.

1. One Noun	
2. Two Adjectives describing #1	
3. Three -ing Verbs about #1	
4. Two Adjectives describing #1; Two for #7	
5. Three -ing Verbs about #7	
6. Two Adjectives describing #7	
7. One Noun (the opposite of #1)	

TLC10605

Extension Activities

1. Discuss the concept of opposites with students. Call out random words that have obvious opposites (hot, cold). As a class, compose diamantes using the two selected words.

2. Find or write several diamantes to hand out to your class. Have students label the part of speech of each word for the diamante by circling nouns, underlining adjectives, and boxing verbs.

3. Cut out pictures of various nouns and place them in an envelope. Have students choose one noun from the envelope about which to write a diamante.

4. Ask students to write their first name at the top of a piece of paper, along with their nickname at the bottom. Then have students fill in the five lines between with words describing themselves.

5. Have students compose one diamante each. As a class, break each poem into nouns, adjectives, and verbs. Draw three boxes on the board, labeling them *nouns*, *adjectives*, and *verbs*.

TLC10605

65

Lune
Low Level

A lune is a three-line poem. Each line has a set number of words. Line 1 has three words; line 2 has five words; and line 3 has three words. Lunes are special because they can say a lot with only 11 words.

1. First, think of a topic for your lune. The poem can be about anything, but keep in mind that you only have 11 words to describe it. Let's write a lune about playing a game.

2. Your first line needs three words. These words can make a sentence or phrase, or they can just be three words about your topic.

   Catch the ball

3. Now, write the second line – it must have five words.

   Catch the ball
   and throw it to me.

4. Finally, write a third line with three words to complete your lune.

   Catch the ball
   and throw it to me.
   I will run.

It can be hard to describe something in 11 words. When you write a lune, try to describe the most important things about your topic.

More Lunes

If I am	(3 words)
the first to home plate,	(5 words)
do I win?	(3 words)

Come over here.	(3 words)
Can I tell you something?	(5 words)
Tag, you're it!	(3 words)

Lune

High Level

The lune is a three-line poem made up of just 11 words (three in line 1, five in line 2, and three in line 3). Lunes are a great example of how poetry can express big ideas in a small amount of space. When writing lunes, try to tell an entire story or express a complete thought, like the poems below.

Who is that?
Not there, but over there.
Made you look!

The sky is
turning purple, blue, and green.
Am I dizzy?

Turtles are slow
because shaking their shells can
hurt their heads.

Lune

Draw a line from the phrase in the first column to the correct phrases in the second and third columns. The three phrases together will complete a lune. The first one has been completed for you.

Only pink pigs	get very lonely out there	under the bridge?
How often does	can fly from barn roof	and stack away!
Cookie crumbs fell	strings are there on a	on the tracks.
Grab the snow,	a troll wash his hair	to barn roof.
Just how many	roll it into three balls,	mice are waiting.
I bet trains	to the kitchen floor where	six-string wooden guitar?

   TLC10605

Lune

The six lunes below have been scrambled. Write the correctly organized lunes on the lines below.

1. you I vote tell my until cannot the are in results.
2. green you pumpkins know all are before Did orange they turn?
3. Be the pear around tree, careful there are near bees all.
4. an race I you can't me elevator beat button in bet.
5. dripping, the Please wax is onto the birthday candle cake hurry!
6. Honestly, and lies, who from stole the no cookies jar my?

1. _____   4. _____

   _____   _____

   _____   _____

2. _____   5. _____

   _____   _____

   _____   _____

3. _____   6. _____

   _____   _____

   _____   _____

Extension Activities

1. Break students into pairs. Have each student write a list of eleven words. All words should be about a similar topic. Instruct students to use each other's lists to write a lune.

2. Have students write a lune about their favorite month or holiday.

3. Find a set of poetry magnets, or make your own poetry word cutouts. Spread them on a table and have students build lunes.

4. Announce a subject to your class. Call on students to supply either one line or an entire lune.

5. Let students choose a topic that interests them. Have students research the topics online or in an encyclopedia and craft a lune about it. Students should present their lunes to the class.

TLC10605

Lyrics
Low Level

Lyrics are the words and lines that make up poems. A lyric has a special sound, like music. Lyrics are what make a poem different from a sentence. Lyrics are especially good for describing special moments, feelings, and ideas. There isn't really a best way to write lyrics – everybody has their own way of making them! The poems below rhyme, but lyrics don't have to rhyme.

Score!

I run this way and that way,
I time it just right.
I get close to the goalie.
He is ready to fight.

He watches my moves
and thinks he knows best.
But I've got a trick,
better than the rest.

I pass to my teammate,
He passes back to me.
I pass to him once more,
He charges for the goalie.

As the goalie awaits the kick,
My teammate passes to me again.
The goalie has no time to save it,
I've already kicked it in!

Mommy

She tucks me in at night
and hugs me when I'm sad.
I tell her school stories.
They make her glad.

She wakes me with a whisper,
It's breakfast time.

She pulls the covers down,
Out I climb.

She waits for me at the bus stop.
All day I have missed her so.
"I love you," I tell her.
"I just want you to know."

TLC10605

71

Lyrics
High Level

Lyrics are the language found in poems. More than simple phrases or sentences, lyrics are strong expressions or descriptions of events, emotions, and ideas. Lyrics are often used to describe abstract ideas. They don't need to follow all the rules of punctuation and grammar. They have a special rhythm and sound.

My Balloon

Last night I dreamt of a white balloon.
It slipped from my fingers.
And was gone too soon.

This made me think of things I miss.
Like my first best friend,
and my grandmother's kiss.

I looked for my balloon in trees nearby.
But I knew it wasn't there.
Some things are meant to fly.

Like airplanes, and the Wright brothers,
who made the first flight.
What if they'd listened to the doubts of others?

They might've missed their
chance to try, to fly,
to take others into the air.

So I'm glad my balloon moved on.
For what wonders it might see
Before the light of dawn.

TLC10605

Lyrics

Circle the song title that best describes each set of lyrics.

With a wave of his wand, out jumps the rabbit.
Making things appear is his famous habit.

The Pirate   The Magician   The Princess

In a tall tower, she waits to be freed.
One brave prince is all she'll need.

The Ant   The Spider   The Princess

He works his six legs morning and night.
When his mound is complete, it's quite a sight!

The Pirate   The Ant   The Magician

On the open seas he likes to roam.
He steals treasure, and has no home.

The Pirate   The Magician   The Spider

Crisscross across the sky,
She patterns a trap for the next coming fly.

The Ant   The Spider   The Princess

Lyrics

Choose two of your favorite songs. Listen closely to their lyrics and music. What do they make you think about? Write new lyrics to the songs on the lines below. Your songs can be about anything. Give your new songs original titles.

Title: _____   Title: _____

_____

_____

_____

_____

_____

_____

_____

_____

_____

Extension Activities

1. Bring in instrumental music to play for your students. Let students either sing or write lyrics for the music.

2. Provide the lyrics to some common songs, such as *Mary Had a Little Lamb* or *Twinkle, Twinkle Little Star*. Have students create new lyrics and titles for these tunes. You might provide a topic to get them started.

3. Give students basic instruments (recorders, drums, etc.). Encourage some students to make music while the others create and sing original lyrics. Encourage students to be creative.

4. Gather the class into a circle for a round of ABC Improv, either on a predetermined topic or of the first student's choice. Starting with A, one student says a complete sentence beginning with an A word. The student to his right or left then says a complete sentence beginning with a B word, based on the previous sentence. And so forth. Encourage students to use poetic devices if possible, such as the lyrical use of emotion, or rhyme, alliteration, etc. *Example: All I really want is a box of candy. But there's more to life than candy. Candy only makes things better for a minute. Donuts, on the other hand, last longer and taste better.*

5. Cut out song lyrics on small pieces of paper. Mix the lyrics in a bag and have each student grab one. Have students write a poem based on the lyric.

Occasional Poetry
Low Level

An occasional poem is about a special event, like a birthday or holiday. Occasional poems describe the event by painting word pictures and expressing feelings.

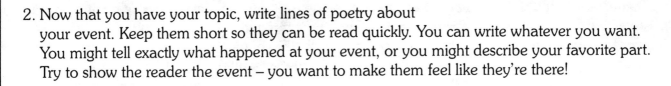

1. First, choose an event about which you want to write. Try to pick something that you really enjoy or remember well. Let's write an occasional poem about a holiday:

   Halloween

2. Now that you have your topic, write lines of poetry about your event. Keep them short so they can be read quickly. You can write whatever you want. You might tell exactly what happened at your event, or you might describe your favorite part. Try to show the reader the event – you want to make them feel like they're there!

   I want to be
   Something big.
   A bumblebee,
   Or a pig.

3. Your occasional poem can be short or long. Keep writing until you've said everything you want to say about the event. When you're finished, a reader should be able to describe the event, even if they weren't there.

My Costume

I want to be
Something big.
A bumblebee,
Or a pig.

Neither will do,
Both are small.
Think of the zoo,
Something tall.

Maybe a bear
With large paws,
Covered in hair,
With wide jaws.

On Halloween
I will growl
And look real mean
With my scowl.

Occasional Poetry

High Level

Occasional poems are about special events. When you write an occasional poem, you want to describe the event as vividly as possible. You can choose whichever aspect of the event you have the most to say about – what happened, how it made you feel, why it's so important. Occasional poems are a fantastic way to record memories. Notice how the poem below uses language to paint a clear picture of Halloween night.

Halloween Sights

What will I be this year?
A ghost? A bear? A princess?
I don't want to cause fear,
So I will just wear a dress.

This one is pink and bright.
Yes, it is the perfect one!
The red dress wasn't right.
I think pink is just more fun!

The sun is setting now.
It is time to walk door to door.
I hear a cat's meow,
and see colored costumes galore.

A brown bird and a worm,
a superhero in the sky.
The one begins to squirm,
the other pretends to fly.

As the pairs walk by us,
each one dressed in something new,
my big brother, Prince Gus,
says "Why, hello" and "Adieu."

Candy fills up our sacks,
I stare deep inside and see
Chocolate, cookies, gum packs,
and more. All just for me!

Occasional Poetry

Number the pictures below in the correct order. Give the poem a title.
Hint: The poem has an *abab rhyme scheme*.

Title: _____

I give hugs and cheer.

_____

I find my seat.

_____

It is time to eat.

_____

The family is here.

_____

78

TLC10605

Name _____   Date _____

Occasional Poetry

Cut out the lines of poetry below. Organize them correctly and paste them on another piece of paper to create an occasional poem. Give the poem a title and decorate it.

Quietly I say thanks, for
I'm truly blessed.

They are colorful, yes, but
where are the meats?

Come on people, could this
take any longer?

There are rolls and potatoes
and gravy brown.

The table is set and
everyone is here.

But the people around me
are what matter.

I see faces now, instead of
turkey fully dressed.

The bird has arrived. Now
we can all sit down.

With each passing platter,
I feel my hunger.

So tasty, I think I could
clean each platter.

I feast my eyes first, and
then I fill my plate.

I see the corn, cranberries,
green beans, and beets.

I take a deep breath. I
can no longer wait.

Oh boy, surely dinnertime
is drawing near.

Extension Activities

1. Divide the class into pairs. Have students take turns giving verbal hints about an occasion and guessing the occasion. (For instance: It's cold outside. I wake up early. I left cookies out the night before. [Christmas]) Or, students can draw hints for each other.

2. Have students write letters to family or friends describing an occasion.

3. Direct students to fold a piece of construction paper in fourths. With a specific occasion in mind, students should draw four scenes from the occasion, in the order in which they would occur.

4. Show students several images from a variety of occasions. Include some less obvious images for a greater challenge. Ask students to choose an image and write a poem based on the occasion it represents.

5. Discuss with your class what constitutes an occasion. Brushing one's teeth? Earning an A+? Running a marathon? Brainstorm a list of lesser-known occasions. In pairs, have students write an occasional poem from one of the occasions listed. No holidays or birthdays allowed!

TLC10605

A round is a poem that repeats. Rounds have rhythm, like a song. In fact, *Mary Had a Little Lamb* and *Row, Row, Row Your Boat* are both rounds.

1. First, pick a topic for your round. Rounds are often used to tell about doing something. Let's write one about playing card games.

2. Write lines about your topic. Be sure to repeat words in some of the lines. This will give your poem a musical sound. Try singing your lines out loud to see how they sound.

> Lay, lay, lay the cards
> We can play a game
> You go, I go, you go, I go
> Back and forth, the same

3. Continue writing lines about your topic until you've said all you want to say.

Card Games

Lay, lay, lay the cards
We can play a game
You go, I go, you go, I go
Back and forth, the same.

Grab, grab, grab the cards
We can play again
Your turn, my turn, your turn, my turn
This time, who will win?

Forts

Stack, stack, stack the pillows
So they make a wall
Please be careful, please be careful
So they do not fall.

Take, take, take the sheet
Throw it to this side
Build a fort, build a fort
Let's all get inside.

Round
High Level

Rounds are musical poems that repeat. These repetitions show how musical poetry can be. You can repeat whichever words or lines you like. Try chanting or singing some of your poetry, even if you didn't mean for it to be musical – you might be surprised!

A Cake for You and Me

Spray, spray, spray the pan
So it does not burn
Heat the oven, heat the oven
Let's all take a turn.

Beat, beat, beat the batter
Until it is just right
Bake it, bake it, bake it, bake it
For a sweet delight.

A Winter Treat

Scoop, scoop, scoop the cocoa
The chocolate looks so sweet
Pour the milk, pour the milk
Now it's time to heat.

Stir, stir, stir the drink
Be careful, it is hot
Sip it slowly, sip it slowly
Let's make another pot.

TLC10605

Round

Fill in the blanks with words from the bank to complete the rounds.

Swat, swat, swat the fly

How does he move so _____?

This way, that way, this way, that way

How long will he last?

Watch, watch, watch the cat

She pounces here and there

Pick her up, pick her up

No, I wouldn't _____.

_____, water, water the flowers

My mom will be so proud.

Pick one, pick one, pick one, pick one

I hope I am allowed.

Rake, rake, rake the _____

They're falling from the trees

Oh no, oh no, _____, oh no

Here comes a sudden breeze.

fast
dare
water
leaves
oh no

Round

Complete the second half of each round. Use your imagination and have fun!

Mop, mop, mop the floor
I do not like to clean

_____

_____

_____

Dust, dust, dust the wood
I really want to stop

_____

_____

_____

Search, search, search the cupboard
Which treat will I pick?

_____

_____

_____

Raise, raise, raise my hand
It's my turn to go

_____

_____

Extension Activities

1. Place the words to a common round on display and sing the round together. Then divide the class into two parts and have each part begin singing at a different time (as in a canon).

2. Point out the one-syllable action words in *Row, Row, Row Your Boat*. Construct a list on the board of other one-syllable action words. Then construct a list of possible nouns. Have students pair verbs and nouns to create new rounds.

3. Pair students up and assign each pair a topic. Students should fold and tear a piece of notebook paper into fourths, and on each fourth write one line of a round. All four pieces should make a complete round. Have students swap and solve the other's round.

4. Take students on a short recess to the playground of your school. Together compile a list of all the rounds one could sing during recess. *For example: Climb, climb, climb the tree. Be careful not to fall. Up, up, up you go. This tree is really tall.*

5. Write a verb on the flat side of a milk cap. Make enough for each pair of students to have one. Have a student from each pair select a milk cap at random. Each pair should glue the cap to a sheet of a paper and write a round using the verb. Have students cut their papers into circles and decorate based on the poem. Hang the rounds in the classroom.

Skeltonic Poetry
Low Level

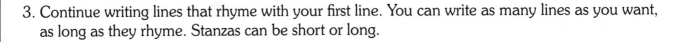

Skeltonic poetry is all about rhyming. Each stanza (group of lines) is made up of rhyming lines. Skeltonic poetry can be about anything at all – all you have to do is start writing!

1. Select a topic about which you want to write. How about horse riding?

2. Write a line of poetry about your topic.

> I want to ride a horse

3. Continue writing lines that rhyme with your first line. You can write as many lines as you want, as long as they rhyme. Stanzas can be short or long.

> I want to ride a horse
> On a forest course.

4. Write as many stanzas as you like on your topic until your skeltonic poem is finished!

I want to ride a horse
On a forest course.

From place to place,
We will race.
Hold on, just in case.

I feel like I could fly,
Sitting up this high
And watching the trees go by.

Is it okay
If I do not know the way?
The horse lets out a *neigh*
What did he say?

He stops on the track
I guess it is time to go back.

86

Skeltonic Poetry
High Level

Skeltonic poetry is made up of stanzas (groups) of rhyming lines. Each stanza is made up of rhyming lines, and can be as short or long as you want to make it. Skeltonic poetry doesn't always need to be planned out. Sometimes it's best to free write and see what comes out! Keep in mind that you can always revisit a poem and make it better.

Thoughts on Fishing

I have only one wish
To go to the lake and catch a fish
Then take it home and make a dish

See the worm fly through the air
The fish below will start to stare
But only one will dare
I know it sounds unfair

The one who bites the hook
Will wish he'd had another look

He thought he was the winner
But now he is my dinner

Should I let the fish die?
Why?

He didn't know the worm was fake
Or that his life was at stake
Now I have a decision to make

The line is thin
I will cut it and throw him in
So he can swim again
Away goes his fin

Skeltonic Poetry

Follow the rhymes through the maze to complete a skeltonic poem.

Start

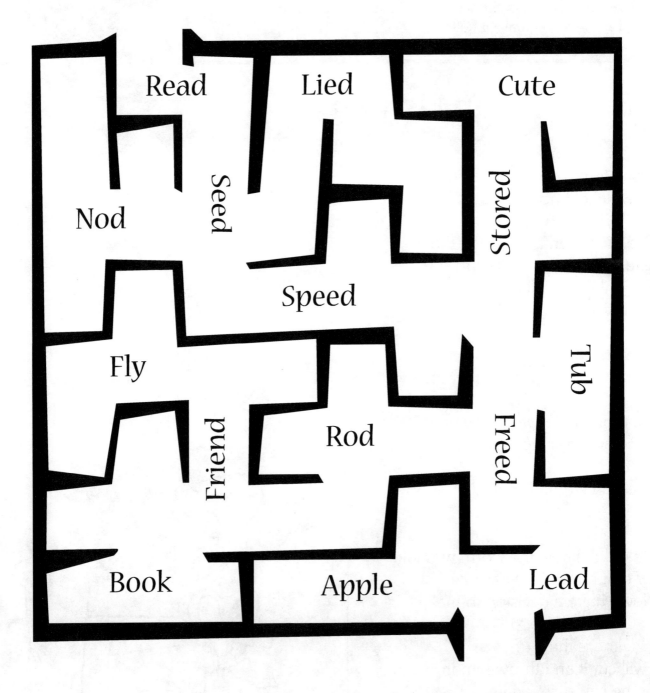

Read   Lied   Cute

Seed

Nod

Stored

Speed

Fly

Tub

Friend   Rod   Freed

Book   Apple   Lead

Finish

TLC10605

Name _____   Date _____

Skeltonic Poetry

Fill in the missing words of the skeltonic poem below.
Then write another stanza to finish the poem.

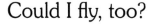

I wonder _____

I stare at the sky

Looking up so _____

At the clouds floating _____

And the birds as they _____.

Could I fly, too?

That's all I want to _____

Just fly into the _____.

I'd be alone up _____

But I wouldn't care.

I'd befriend the birds

Though they speak no _____.

_____

_____

_____

Extension Activities

1. Have students take turns writing things they see outside. Use some of the words to write a skeltonic poem on the board.

2. After altering some rhymes so that they are incorrect, read aloud a long skeltonic poem. Have students walk in a circle, stepping forward when they hear a rhyme and sitting when they hear an error.

3. Show students three unrelated objects. Allow them to pick them up and/or ask questions about them. Then have students write a skeltonic based on the three objects.

4. Challenge your class to a Skeltonathon. Within a certain time frame, each student should attempt to write the longest skeltonic possible. The only rule is that they must use real words.

5. Be a Skeltonic for a day. Tell your students that today your name is *Mrs. Russ Bus*, or *Mr. Wright Kite*. One by one have each student reintroduce themselves to the class. Students are to remember their new full names and use them throughout the day.

TLC10605

Tongue Twister

Low Level

A tongue twister is a group of words that begin with the same letter or sound. Tongue twisters are hard to say. They are usually strange or funny.

1. Start a tongue twister by writing a word – any word. How about:

     blue

2. Next, think of more words that begin with the same letter or sound. They can be related to the first word, but they don't have to be. Sometimes, a good tongue twister doesn't make any sense.

     blue blossoms bloomed

Try to say your words five times fast. If you have any trouble, you've created a great tongue twister!

More Tongue Twisters

Coral crayons colored.

Green grubs groaned.

Sherry shined several silver shoes.

Do dust Dan's dirty desk.

Tongue Twisters
High Level

Tongue twisters are series of words beginning with the same letter or sound – like long, funny alliterations. A good tongue twister will be very difficult to say out loud, and might inspire lots of laughter. Tongue twisters aren't always fun and games, though. Some serious poetry can come from them. Consider the clear, memorable images created by the following tongue twisters.

Purple-painted pianos piped a pretty tune.

Red rainbow rays ran in different ways.

Silver stained statues stood still in the sun.

One wise worm wiggled into the warm ground.

Two tiny turtles tripped on the tree trunk.

Three thirsty bees silently stung someone's thumb.

Four forgetful frogs found food from last fall.

Five frisky felines fought for the last lick.

Six sick salmon swam swiftly upstream.

TLC10605

Tongue Twisters

Connect the words of the tongue twister to reveal a hidden picture.

Tiny

1 ●

tan
●
2

3 ●
tuna

to
●
5

try
●
4

7 ●
treats

trap
● 6

Tongue Twisters

Fill in the chart below. The first row asks for words beginning with the letter **F**, the second row is for words beginning with **R**, and the last row is for words beginning with **S**. After completing the chart, write three tongue twisters with the words. Include additional words to make the twisters even more difficult to say.

	Adjectives	Nouns	Verbs
F		fish	
R	red		
S			slide

1. _____

   _____

2. _____

   _____

3. _____

   _____

TLC10605

Extension Activities

1. Cut several two- or three-word tongue twisters into individual word cards. In small groups, have students play a memory game with them. After shuffling the word cards, students should place the cards face down and take turns flipping two (or three) of them over. The goal is to turn over all of the tongue twister cards for a particular letter in one turn.

2. Create letter specific bingo cards at print-bingo.com. Include nouns, verbs, and adjectives. In pairs or separately, have students cover words as you call them out. Whoever calls *Bingo* must read their winning words aloud. Write the words on the board and use them to create a tongue twister.

3. Have students write a tongue twister on a piece of paper. Then have students cut the sentence apart, word-by-word, and place the pieces in an envelope. On the outside of the envelope, students should draw a picture that illustrates the completed tongue twister. Instruct students to exchange envelopes and organize each other's tongue twisters.

4. Cut white construction paper into various shapes. Distribute one shape to each student. Have students write one tongue twister about their shape. Encourage students to be creative with their tongue twisters.

5. Provide the words to common tongue twisters. Let students try saying them aloud. As a class alter the tongue twisters to create new meanings.

Triplet
Low Level

A triplet is a set of three lines of poetry. These lines do not have to rhyme, but they usually do. You can rhyme them in any combination.

1. First, choose a topic. It should be pretty simple, since you only have three lines to describe it. Let's write a triplet about getting hurt.

2. Decide if you want to use rhyme in your triplet. You can rhyme your lines in any combination, or not at all. It's up to you. We'll use an *abb rhyme scheme* – the second and third lines will rhyme.

3. Write lines of poetry about your topic. If you chose a rhyme scheme, be sure to use it.

   I hurt myself.
   I was walking to slow
   And stubbed my baby toe.

4. If you like, you can write an entire poem of triplets! Just keep writing groups of three lines about your topic. You can use the same rhyme scheme for the whole poem, or change it throughout, like the poem below.

Ouch!

I hurt myself.	(a)	Someone please help me.	(a)
I was walking too slow	(b)	This is so scary.	(a)
And stubbed my baby toe.	(b)	Does it hurt? Very!	(a)
Now what do I do?	(a)	Grandma covers my cut.	(a)
Grab a soft tissue?	(a)	She knew what to do.	(b)
Wipe the blood away?	(b)	Back outside I go!	(c)
My, oh my,	(a)		
Does it sting!	(b)		
I might cry.	(a)		

TLC10605

Triplet
High Level

Triplets are three-line stanzas with or without a rhyme scheme. You might rhyme the first two lines, all of the lines, or none of them. You can combine a group of triplets into a longer poem. Triplets show how rhyme can impact poetry, but they also show that it isn't necessary for a poem to rhyme. One of the best things about poetry is that anything goes – it's all up to the poet.

A Friday with a Friend

I want to have a slumber party.   (a)
Please will you come and stay?   (b)
I promise we will play.   (b)

Do you like to bake?   (a)
We can make a cake.   (a)
We will eat it all.   (b)

What will we do outside?   (a)
I will stand and count,   (b)
You find a place to hide.   (a)

Do you like cartoons,   (a)
And ice cream with spoons,   (a)
And popping balloons?   (a)

We will have fun.   (a)
My family is nice.   (b)
They hope you come over.   (c)

Triplet

Cut out the pictures below. Use one picture to correctly complete each triplet. Paste the answer in the box provided.

What travels faster
than all of the cars,
in the air, below the _____?

A salty body of waves,
sharks, and _____.
I am different than dry land.

Orange and round, with many _____,
A face is all I need.
Who will carve me?

Who needs _____
out on the plain,
for his fields of grain?

 rain

 seeds

 stars

 sand

TLC10605

Triplet

Circle the title that best describes each triplet.

We visit him in an office or at a hospital.
He checks our hearts, our teeth, and eyes.
He helps us live long because he is wise.

Police Officer   Doctor   Mail Carrier

With a stamp and a smile, we greet her each day.
She hands us a letter, and takes the others away.
She will return again, but not on Sunday!

Police Officer   Mail Carrier   Firefighter

When there is smoke and flames, he soon will arrive.
While others gather around, he rushes inside.
He saves families from danger, making sure all survive!

Mail Carrier   Teacher   Firefighter

If crime is in our city, she's the first to find out.
If ever we need help, she's there without a doubt.
A protector and a friend, for us she will defend.

Police Officer   Doctor   Teacher

There is one person, different from all the rest.
She helps me read and write, and study for a test.
Without her I would never learn to be my very best.

Doctor   Teacher   Firefighter

Extension Activities

1. Read students a book synopsis. Ask each to write a triplet based on what they understand the book to be about. Allow them to choose whichever rhyme pattern they prefer.

2. Read Dr. Seuss to your students, or have them read a story individually. Explain the silly, nonsensical nature of Seuss's use of rhyme. Then have students write triplets with their names. They can use full names, first or last, or simply the letters of their names. *For example:*
   My name is J-u-l-i-a
   And I just want to say,
   I love pizza!

3. Have each student draw and color a picture. Then have students swap pictures. Each student should write a triplet based on the picture.

4. Place a long list of familiar rhyming words on display. Before revealing the list, explain that students should read over it and raise their hands whenever they've decided on three words they can use to make a triplet. Whoever raises his or her hand first recites a triplet to the class.

5. Provide each student with a postcard. Have students imagine they're on a trip and want to share with family something they've seen, tasted, heard, or smelled. On the blank side of the postcard, have students write a triplet about it.

TLC10605

Answer Key

Page 7

Page 8
Answers may vary slightly.
My mother makes marvelous meatballs.
Susan's socks smell so stinky.
Laura lost Lindsey's luggage.

Page 11
D
C
A
E
B

Page 12
hungry, kitchen
cold, snowman
mirror, looking
stare, *eyes*
high, sun
coconuts, mouth

Page 15
The moon is a flashlight.
I am a turtle.
My brother is an animal.
Your hands are sandpaper.
Sandy is a lobster.
This room is an oven.

Page 16
Answers will vary.
kite
flower
snow

Page 19
N   N
S   S
S   N

Page 20
(Meanings may vary)
The sky is as big as an ocean. (The sky is large.)
Ballerinas move across the floor like feathers. (Ballerinas are graceful.)
Careful, the pencil is sharp as a tack. (The pencil is sharp.)
Your teapot whistles like a train. (Your teapot is loud.)
Her nose was as red as Rudolph's. (Her nose was very red.)
He bites his nails like a dog chewing a bone. (He bites his nails eagerly.)

Page 23

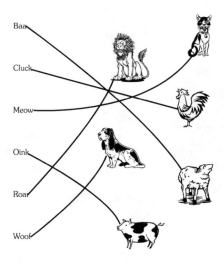

Baa
Cluck
Meow
Oink
Roar
Woof

Page 24

roar; oink
beeping; knocking
hummed; whacked
gurgling; clucking
zap; tick-tock
rumble; sizzle
snort; meow

Page 27

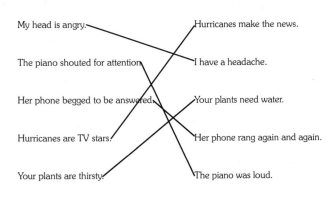

My head is angry.
The piano shouted for attention.
Her phone begged to be answered.
Hurricanes are TV stars.
Your plants are thirsty.

Hurricanes make the news.
I have a headache.
Your plants need water.
Her phone rang again and again.
The piano was loud.

Page 28

Answers will vary.

Page 33

Brushed
Lights
Almost
Nothing
Keep
Excited
Tell

Page 34

Answers will vary.

Page 38

The Zoo

Ants, birds, cheetahs, ducks,
elephant, flamingo,
giraffe, hippo,
insect, jaguar, kangaroo, lion,
monkey, noisy,
otter, panda, quiet, rabbit,
seals, tigers,
ugly, vicious, wolf,
eXciting,
yak, zebra

Page 39

Answers will vary.

Page 43

Wake up early
Pack my backpack
Sit at my desk

Are funny
Are smart
Are helpful

Is friendly
Is soft
Is fast

Watch cartoons
Eat pancakes
Play games

My Dog
Saturdays
My Friends
Mondays

TLC10605

Page 44

How to Climb a Tree
Start by grabbing the lowest branch with both hands.
Find a place for your toe.
Now lift yourself on top of the branch.
Rest before climbing higher!

How to Skip a Rock
Start with a flat and smooth stone.
Hold the stone like a Frisbee.
Squat down close to the shore.
Aim just above the water and throw!

Page 48

small, play
bell, sweet
thin, white
jar, pop

Page 49

Rita Ray
Had nothing to say.
She tried to shout,
But nothing came out
Birdy Brown
Was known around town
For his beautiful tune
That made others swoon
Johnny Stop Staring
Had a habit of glaring.
His eyes were blurry and red,
As he never put them to bed
Willy Watch Out
Was a private scout.
He uncovered crimes and lies
While in perfect disguise

Page 53

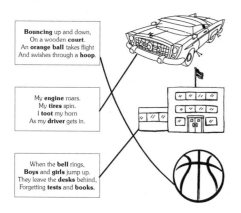

Page 54

Answers will vary.

Page 58

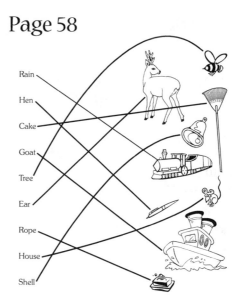

Page 59

Answers will vary.

Page 63

Poem may appear in reverse order
Pupil
Young, Curious
Reading, Talking, Thinking
Doing what is best
Playing, Writing, Asking
Tired, Excited
Student

Page 64

Answers will vary.

Page 68

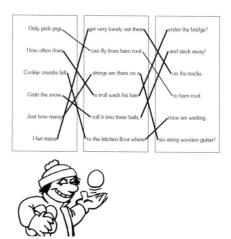

Page 69

1. I cannot tell
   you my vote until the
   results are in.
2. Did you know
   all pumpkins are green before
   they turn orange?
3. Be careful near
   the pear tree, there are
   bees all around.
4. I bet you
   can't beat me in an
   elevator button race.
5. Please hurry, the
   candle wax is dripping onto
   the birthday cake!
6. Honestly, and no
   lies, who stole the cookies
   from my jar?

Page 73

The Magician
The Princess
The Ant
The Pirate
The Spider

Page 74

Answers will vary.

Page 78

Page 79

The table is set and everyone is here.
Oh boy, surely dinnertime is drawing near.
With each passing platter, I feel my hunger.
Come on people, could this take any longer?
I see the corn, cranberries, green beans, and beets.
They are colorful, yes, but where are the meats?
The bird has arrived. Now we can all sit down.
There are rolls and potatoes and gravy brown.
I feast my eyes first, and then I fill my plate.
I take a deep breath. I can no longer wait.
So tasty, I think I could clean each platter.
But the people around me are what matter.
I see faces now, instead of turkey fully dressed.
Quietly I say thanks, for I'm truly blessed.

Page 83

fast
dare
Water
leaves
oh no

Page 84

Answers will vary.

Page 88

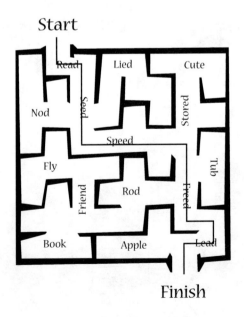

TLC10605

Page 89

Words may vary
why
high
by
fly
do
blue
there
words
Last stanza will vary

Page 93

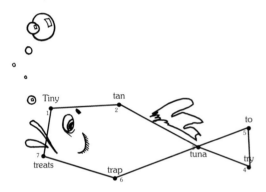

Page 94

Answers will vary.

Page 98

What travels faster
than all of the cars,
in the air, below the _____?

stars

A salty body of waves,
sharks, and _____.
I am different than dry land.

sand

Orange and round, with many _____,
A face is all I need.
Who will carve me?

seeds

Who needs _____
out on the plain,
for his fields of grain?

rain

Page 99

Doctor
Mail Carrier
Firefighter
Police Officer
Teacher

Poetry Ideas

Poetry Ideas

Poetry Ideas

TLC10605